ARTIST TRANSCRIPTIONS SAXOPHONE

THE Frank Morgan COLLECTION

CONTENTS

Cover Photo by Ed Seiz

ISBN 0-7935-9321-2

HAL•LEONARD®
CORPORATION
7777 W. BLUEMOUND RD. P.O. BOX 13819 MILWAUKEE, WI 53213

Visit Hal Leonard Online at
www.halleonard.com

Frank Morgan

SELECTED DISCOGRAPHY

All the Things You Are, My One and Only Love, The Nearness of You –
Love, Lost and Found—Telarc CD-83374; 3/7+9/95

Easy Living – Easy Living—Original Jazz Classics OJC-833;
12/14+15/86

Half Nelson – Lament—Contemporary CCD-14021; 4/86

How Deep Is the Ocean – Major Changes—Contemporary CCD-14039; 4/87

In a Sentimental Mood, Mood Indigo, We Three Blues – Mood Indigo—
Antilles 791 320; 6/27+28/89

It Might As Well Be Spring – Listen to the Dawn—Antilles 314 518;
4/19+11/27/93

My Old Flame – Introducing Frank Morgan—LP: GNP 12;
CD-GNPD 904; 1955

A Night in Tunisia – Yardbird Suite—Contemporary CCD-14045;
1/10+11/88

While the Gettin's Good Blues, You've Changed – You Must Believe in Spring—
Antilles 314 512 570; 3/10+11/92

Frank Morgan

The word that may best describe alto saxophonist Frank Morgan is "survivor." A disciple of Charlie Parker, Morgan spent most of his adult life in prisons, finally emerging in 1985 to live up to the greatness originally predicted for him. One critic called it "one of the most remarkable comebacks in the history of music."

Born in Minneapolis on December 23, 1933 to guitarist Stanley Morgan and his fourteen-year-old wife Geraldine, Frank himself was playing the guitar at the age of two. But it was age seven that Frank heard the sound that changed his life. Visiting his father in Detroit on vacation from school in Milwaukee, where he had been living with his father's family, Frank accompanied Stanley to the Paradise Theatre, where the Jay McShann band was the feature attraction. When Charlie Parker took his first solo, Frank decided then and there that he wanted to play the alto saxophone. Stanley, who had played with Parker in Kansas City, introduced Frank to his new idol after the concert, and the next day saxophonists Wardell Gray and Teddy Edwards, from Howard McGhee's band, picked out Frank's first horn: on the recommendation of Bird, a clarinet.

By 1947, Stanley had moved to LA and opened a club on Central Avenue, LA's equivalent of 52nd Street. Frank, now playing alto, visited Stanley and found himself in jam sessions with LA's leading beboppers. The following year he moved to LA, and by age seventeen Frank was in the house band at the Club Alabam, playing behind legends like Josephine Baker and Billie Holiday. Charlie Parker took Frank under his wing and the two would play together whenever Bird visited LA. Hailed as "the new Bird," and under the impression that "the heroin and the bebop and the whole lifestyle thing went together," Frank soon began using himself. Upon learning this, Bird expressed his anger and disappointment, but Frank was hooked. In 1955, the year of Bird's death, Frank cut his first album as a leader, with a band that included Gray, Conte Candoli and Carl Perkins. Shortly after that, instead of going to New York with the band, Frank went to jail for the first time.

For the next three decades, Morgan lived a life of nonviolent crime to support his habit. Twenty-two of those years were spent behind bars. He read, played chess and continued to play jazz in excellent prison bands with other musician/addicts like Art Pepper and Frank Butler, but to the above-ground jazz world he was a forgotten man. Not until 1985, after being rediscovered by critic Leonard Feather, and under the positive influence of artist (and later spouse) Rosalinda Kolb, did he finally break the cycle of addiction, crime, and imprisonment, and return to the jazz scene full time. Following the release of his first post-comeback recording, "Easy Living," he finally made his long-postponed New York debut at the Village Vanguard, with lines around the block, glowing reviews, and a level of mainstream media attention rarely bestowed upon a jazz artist.

In 1987, Morgan played himself in an off-Broadway musical based on his life in prison. The presentation lasted ten performances, all sold out. There were plans to bring the show to Broadway, but Frank declined. He preferred to play his horn. Since then he has recorded a dozen more critically-acclaimed albums as a leader and led a busy touring schedule, playing at clubs, festivals, and concert halls around the world, and sharing his story with inmates, recovering addicts, and "at risk" youth. In August of 1998, on the way to a festival in Flint, Michigan, Morgan suffered a stroke on the left side of his brain. Following an intensive six-month rehabilitation, he made his second comeback at Blues Alley in Washington, D.C. with Sir Roland Hanna. A tour with Art Farmer soon followed, and the word was out – "Frank's back!" – again, playing passionate bebop and lyrical ballads as only Frank Morgan can.

All the Things You Are

from VERY WARM FOR MAY

Lyrics by OSCAR HAMMERSTEIN II
Music by JEROME KERN

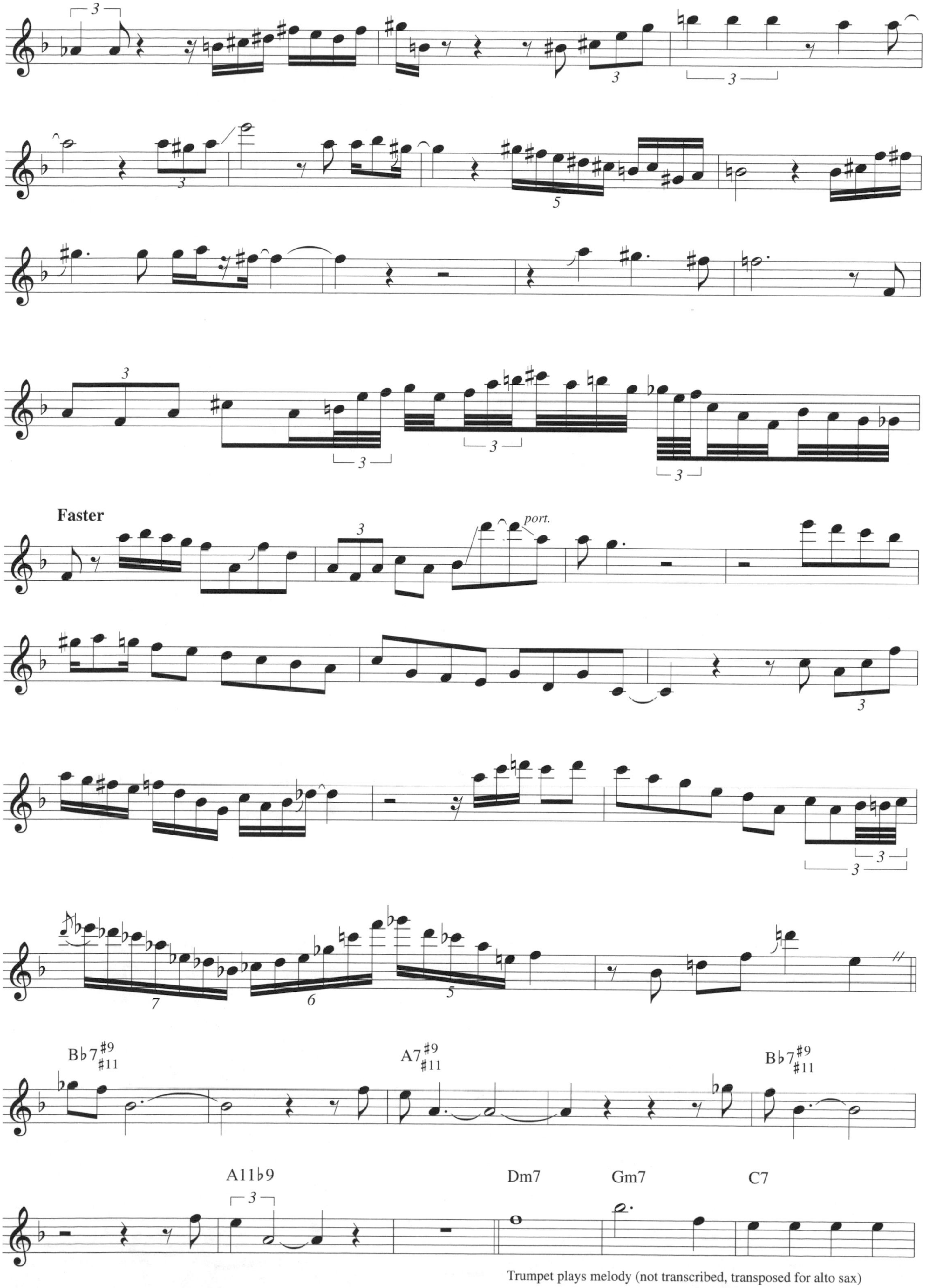
Faster
port.
B♭7#9 #11
A7#9 #11
B♭7#9 #11
A11♭9
Dm7
Gm7
C7
Trumpet plays melody (not transcribed, transposed for alto sax)

9

Half Nelson

Words and Music by MILES DAVIS

* The piece is written in double-time

Easy Living
Theme from the Paramount Picture EASY LIVING
Words and Music by LEO ROBIN and RALPH RAINGER

How Deep Is the Ocean
(How High Is the Sky)

Words and Music by IRVING BERLIN

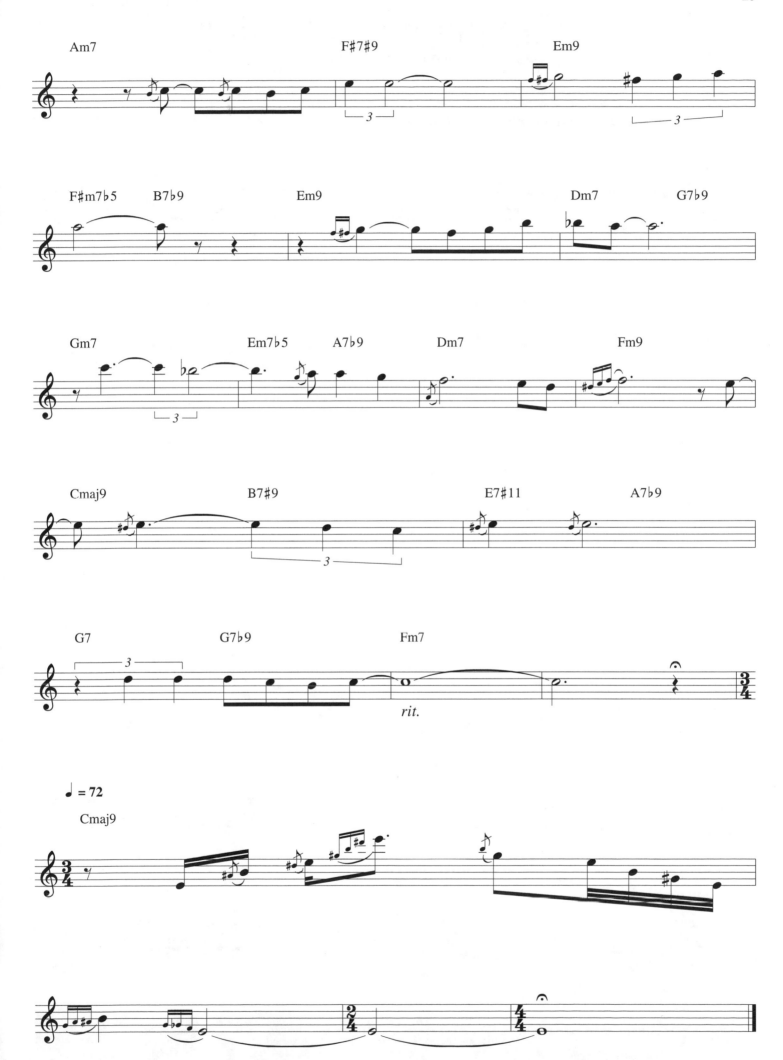

In a Sentimental Mood

By DUKE ELLINGTON

* Free rhythmically

It Might As Well Be Spring

from STATE FAIR

Lyrics by OSCAR HAMMERSTEIN II
Music by RICHARD RODGERS

Mood Indigo
from SOPHISTICATED LADIES
Words and Music by DUKE ELLINGTON, IRVING MILLS and ALBANY BIGARD

My Old Flame
from the Paramount Picture BELLE OF THE NINETIES
Words and Music by ARTHUR JOHNSTON and SAM COSLOW

My One and Only Love

Words by ROBERT MELLIN
Music by GUY WOOD

Note: For ease of reading, chord changes are notated in ♭'s where appropriate.

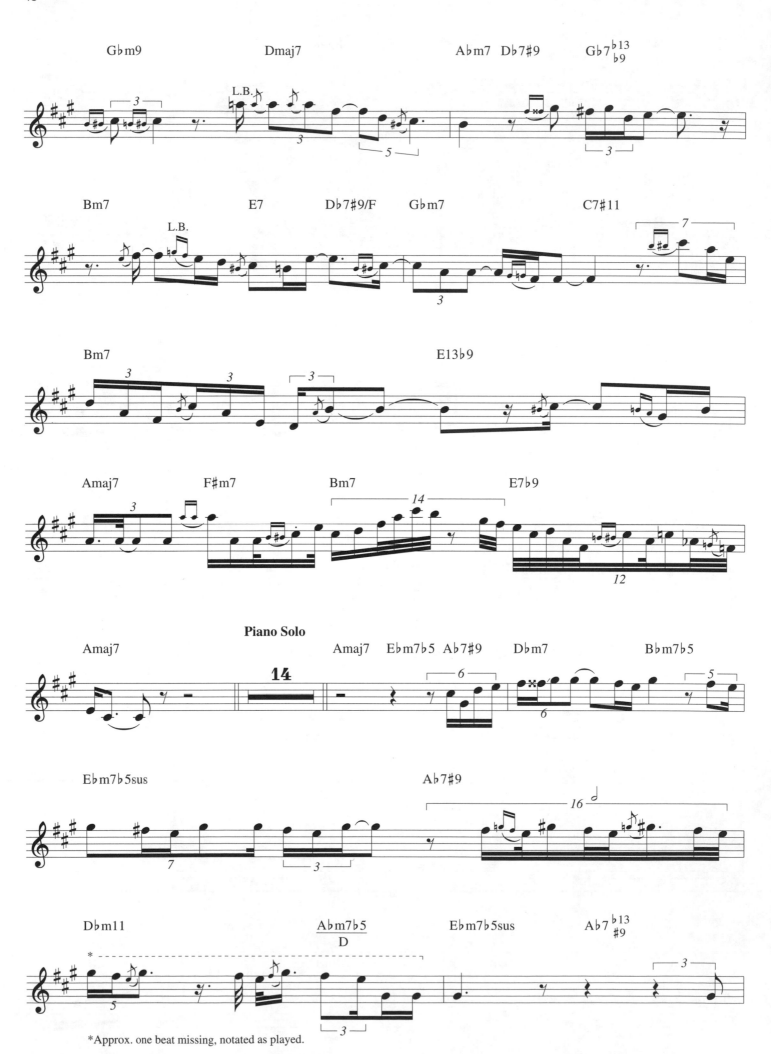

*Approx. one beat missing, notated as played.

The Nearness of You
from the Paramount Picture ROMANCE IN THE DARK

Words by NED WASHINGTON
Music by HOAGY CARMICHAEL

52

A Night in Tunisia

Music by JOHN "DIZZY" GILLESPIE and FRANK PAPARELLI

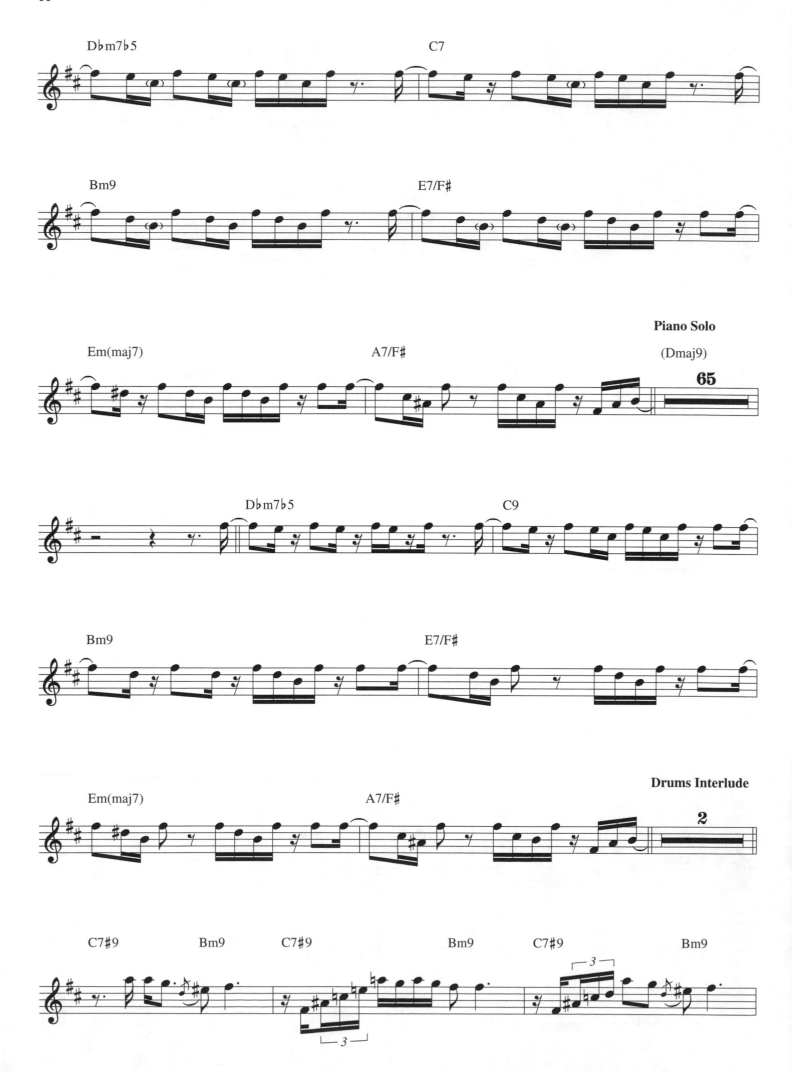

While the Gettin's Good Blues

By FRANK MORGAN and BARRY HARRIS

*50 cents low

You've Changed
Words and Music by BILL CAREY and CARL FISCHER

68

We Three Blues

By FRANK MORGAN

Intro

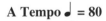

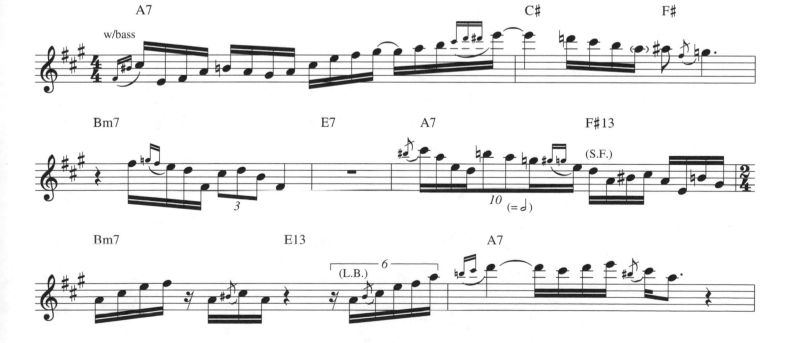

70

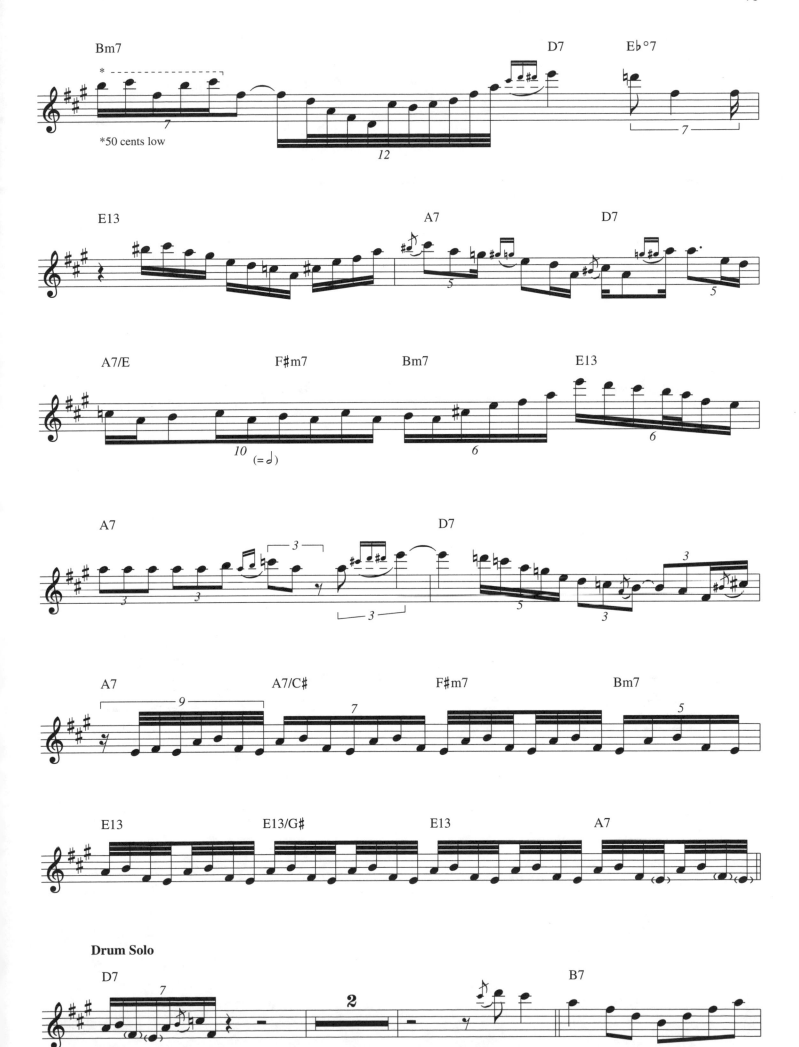

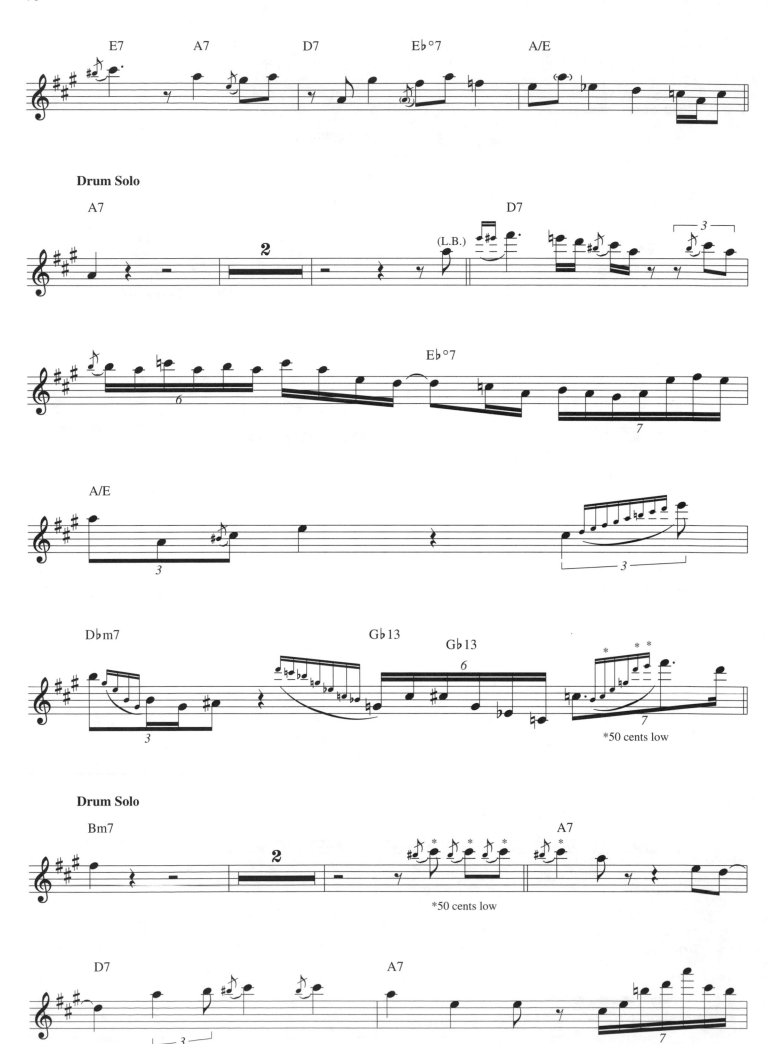

Drum Solo

*50 cents low

*50 cents low

ARTIST TRANSCRIPTIONS

Artist Transcriptions are authentic, note-for-note transcriptions of the hottest artists in jazz, pop, and rock today. These outstanding, accurate arrangements are in an easy-to-read format which includes all essential lines. Artist Transcriptions can be used to perform, sequence or reference.

GUITAR & BASS

The Guitar Book of Pierre Bensusan
00699072.....................................$19.95

Ron Carter – Acoustic Bass
00672331.....................................$16.95

Charley Christian –
The Art of Jazz Guitar
00026704.......................................$6.95

Stanley Clarke Collection
00672307.....................................$19.95

Larry Coryell – Jazz Guitar Solos
00699140.......................................$9.95

Al Di Meola – Cielo E Terra
00604041.....................................$14.95

Al Di Meola –
Friday Night in San Francisco
00660115.....................................$14.95

Al Di Meola – Music, Words, Pictures
00604043.....................................$14.95

Kevin Eubanks Guitar Collection
00672319.....................................$19.95

The Jazz Style of Tal Farlow
00673245.....................................$19.95

Bela Fleck and the Flecktones
00672359 Melody/Lyrics/Chords....$14.95

David Friesen – Departure
00673221.....................................$14.95

David Friesen – Years Through Time
00673253.....................................$14.95

Best Of Frank Gambale
00672336.....................................$22.95

Jim Hall – Jazz Guitar Environments
00699389 Book/CD $19.95

Jim Hall – Exploring Jazz Guitar
00699306.....................................$16.95

Scott Henderson Guitar Book
00699330.....................................$19.95

Allan Holdsworth –
Reaching for the Uncommon Chord
00604049.....................................$14.95

Leo Kottke – Eight Songs
00699215.....................................$14.95

Wes Montgomery – Guitar Transcriptions
00675536.....................................$14.95

Joe Pass Collection
00672353.....................................$14.95

John Patitucci
00673216.....................................$14.95

Django Reinhardt Anthology
00027083.....................................$14.95

The Genius of Django Reinhardt
00026711.....................................$10.95

Django Reinhardt – A Treasury of Songs
00026715.....................................$12.95

John Renbourn – The Nine Maidens,
The Hermit, Stefan and John
00699071.....................................$12.95

Great Rockabilly Guitar Solos
00692820.....................................$14.95

John Scofield – Guitar Transcriptions
00603390.....................................$16.95

Andres Segovia –
20 Studies for the Guitar
00006362 Book/Cassette $14.95

Johnny Smith Guitar Solos
00672374.....................................$14.95

Mike Stern Guitar Book
00673224.....................................$16.95

Mark Whitfield
00672320.....................................$19.95

Jack Wilkins – Windows
00673249.....................................$14.95

Gary Willis Collection
00672337.....................................$19.95

CLARINET

Buddy De Franco Collection
00672423.....................................$19.95

FLUTE

James Newton – Improvising Flute
00660108.....................................$14.95

TROMBONE

J.J. Johnson Collection
00672332.....................................$19.95

TRUMPET

Randy Brecker
00673234.....................................$14.95

The Brecker Brothers...
And All Their Jazz
00672351.....................................$19.95

Best of the Brecker Brothers
00672447.....................................$19.95

Miles Davis – Originals
00672448.....................................$19.95

Miles Davis – Standards
00672450.....................................$19.95

Freddie Hubbard
00673214.....................................$14.95

Tom Harrell Jazz Trumpet
00672382.....................................$19.95

Jazz Trumpet Solos
00672363.......................................$9.95

PIANO & KEYBOARD

Monty Alexander Collection
00672338.....................................$19.95

Kenny Barron Collection
00672318.....................................$22.95

Warren Bernhardt Collection
00672364.....................................$19.95

Billy Childs Collection
00673242.....................................$19.95

Chick Corea – Beneath the Mask
00673225.....................................$12.95

Chick Corea – Elektric Band
00603126.....................................$15.95

Chick Corea – Eye of the Beholder
00660007.....................................$14.95

Chick Corea – Light Years
00674305.....................................$14.95

Chick Corea – Paint the World
00672300.....................................$12.95

Bill Evans Collection
00672365.....................................$19.95

Benny Green Collection
00672329.....................................$19.95

Ahmad Jamal Collection
00672322.....................................$22.95

Jazz Master Classics for Piano
00672354.....................................$14.95

Thelonius Monk – Intermediate
Piano Solos
00672392.....................................$12.95

Jelly Roll Morton – The Piano Rolls
00672433.....................................$12.95

Michel Petrucciani
00673226.....................................$17.95

Bud Powell Classics
00672371.....................................$19.95

André Previn Collection
00672437.....................................$19.95

Joe Sample – Ashes to Ashes
00672310.....................................$14.95

Horace Silver Collection
00672303.....................................$19.95

Art Tatum Collection
00672316.....................................$22.95

Art Tatum Solo Book
00672355.....................................$19.95

Billy Taylor Collection
00672357.....................................$24.95

McCoy Tyner
00673215.....................................$14.95

SAXOPHONE

Julian "Cannonball" Adderly Collection
00673244.....................................$16.95

Michael Brecker
00673237.....................................$16.95

Michael Brecker Collection
00672429.....................................$17.95

The Brecker Brothers...
And All Their Jazz
00672351.....................................$19.95

Best of the Brecker Brothers
00672447.....................................$19.95

Benny Carter Plays Standards
00672315.....................................$22.95

Benny Carter Collection
00672314.....................................$22.95

James Carter Collection
00672394.....................................$19.95

John Coltrane – Giant Steps
00672349.....................................$19.95

John Coltrane Solos
00673233.....................................$22.95

Paul Desmond Collection
00672328.....................................$19.95

Stan Getz
00699375.....................................$14.95

Stan Getz – Bossa Novas – Saxophone
00672377.....................................$16.95

Great Tenor Sax Solos
00673254.....................................$18.95

Joe Henderson – Selections from
"Lush Life" & "So Near So Far"
00673252.....................................$19.95

Best of Joe Henderson
00672330.....................................$22.95

Jazz Master Classics for Tenor Sax
00672350.....................................$18.95

Best Of Kenny G
00673239.....................................$19.95

Kenny G – Breathless
00673229.....................................$19.95

Kenny G – The Moment
00672373.....................................$19.95

Joe Lovano Collection
00672326.....................................$19.95

James Moody Collection – Sax and Flute
00672372.....................................$19.95

The Art Pepper Collection
00672301.....................................$19.95

Sonny Rollins Collection
00672444.....................................$19.95

David Sanborn Collection
00675000.....................................$14.95

Best of David Sanborn
00120891.....................................$14.95

Stanley Turrentine Collection
00672334.....................................$19.95

Ernie Watts Saxophone Collection
00673256.....................................$18.95

FOR MORE INFORMATION, SEE YOUR LOCAL MUSIC DEALER, OR WRITE TO:

HAL•LEONARD®
CORPORATION

7777 W. BLUEMOUND RD. P.O. BOX 13819 MILWAUKEE, WI 53213

Visit our web site for a complete listing of our titles with songlists.
www.halleonard.com

0300